# ZOINKS!
## The Mystery of Forces and Motion!

by Ailynn Collins

CAPSTONE PRESS
a capstone imprint

Published by Capstone Press, an imprint of Capstone
1710 Roe Crest Drive, North Mankato, Minnesota 56003
capstonepub.com

Copyright © 2025 Hanna-Barbera.

SCOOBY-DOO and all related characters and elements are trademarks of and © Hanna-Barbera. (s25)

Library of Congress Cataloging-in-Publication Data is available on the Library of Congress website.

ISBN: 9781669084822 (hardcover)
ISBN: 9781669084778 (paperback)
ISBN: 9781669084785 (ebook PDF)

Summary: Zoom to the skate park with Scooby and the Mystery Inc. gang for a thrilling investigation of forces and motion. Watch as they skate into the physics of speed, balance, and gravity. Filled with zany antics, action-packed discoveries, and dynamic illustrations, this Scooby-Doo! Science Adventure makes learning about physics an exhilarating ride.

Editorial Credits
Editor: Donald Lemke; Designer: Tracy Davies; Media Researcher: Svetlana Zhurkin; Production Specialist: Whitney Schaefer

Image Credits
Getty Images: Cavan Images, 4, duncan1890, 8 (Newton), fcafotodigital, 10, Joe McBride, 5, sonyae, 15, ssj414, 18; Shutterstock: 5 second Studio, 21 (pillow), Alexey Kuznetsov, 25 (top), Alfa Photostudio, 7, AlohaHawaii, 25 (middle), Andrej Antic, 8 (frame), Anton Starikov, 20 (bubble wrap), Artem Sokolov, 16 (straw), bergamont, 8 (apple), Carolyn Franks, 16 (tape), Cartooncux (beaker), cover and throughout, Christos Georghiou, cover (bowling ball and pins), Eky Studio, 16 (twine), Graham Montanari, 16 (balloon), grayjay, 23, HobbitArt (science icons), cover and throughout, joingate, 28, kornnphoto, 12, Lana_L, 20 (egg), Macrovector (skateboard), cover and throughout, Maria Martyshova (background), cover and throughout, matimix, 13, matkub2499, 20 (straws), Mega Pixel, 21 (parachute), Mike Orlov, 26, Monkey Business Images, 24, Naypong Studio, 6, PeopleImages-Yuri A, 29, Photoongraphy, 19, StockPhotosArt, 20 (tape), Stormbreaker Productions, 22, Tyra Yusri, 16 (scissors), udaix, 14 (middle), 17 (balloon), VectorMine, 9, 11, wabeno, 20 (box), WBMUL, 14 (bottom), ZoranOrcik, 27

Any additional websites and resources referenced in this book are not maintained, authorized, or sponsored by Capstone. All product and company names are trademarks™ or registered® trademarks of their respective holders.

# Table of Contents

**INTRODUCTION**
Skateboarding Scooby ............................. 4

**CHAPTER 1**
Motion Mystery ..................................... 6

**CHAPTER 2**
Show of Force ..................................... 18

**CHAPTER 3**
Life in Motion ..................................... 24

**CHAPTER 4**
Physics at Work ................................... 28

Glossary .............................................. 30
Read More ......................................... 31
Internet Sites ..................................... 31
Index .................................................. 32
About the Author ............................... 32

# INTRODUCTION

# Skateboarding Scooby

Scooby-Doo and the Mystery Inc. gang are hanging out at a local skate park. The sun is shining. The air is filled with the sounds of wheels on concrete.

Shaggy and Scooby are trying to skateboard, wobbling and laughing as they go. Daphne and Fred are already quite good at it, smoothly gliding around the park. A few young expert skaters are there too. They show off impressive tricks!

Far out, guys! Those are some out-of-this-world moves!

Actually, Fred, it's all about physics!

Physics is the study of forces and motion. There are many types of motions and forces in play at the skate park. Let's look at forces and motion more closely. OK, gang?

# Motion Mystery

Motion happens when something moves from one place to another. The opposite of motion is stillness.

Walking, running, or riding in the Mystery Machine is motion. Sliding down a ramp on a skateboard is motion too!

Motion needs force. Force is something that causes the motion. A skateboard will not move on its own. It needs a person (or a mystery-solving dog) to push or pull it.

Forces can come from other places as well, like running water or a strong wind. Even **gravity** is a force.

In 1687, a scientist named Sir Isaac Newton published his laws of motion. He asked many questions about how and why things move or stop moving.

His questions led to his three laws of motion. These laws are the building blocks of physics today.

Sir Isaac Newton

# NEWTON'S LAWS OF MOTION

Newton's First Law: An object at rest remains at rest. An object in motion remains in motion.

Newton's Second Law: The **acceleration** of an object depends on the **mass** of the object and the amount of force applied.

Newton's Third Law: For every action, there is an equal and opposite reaction.

## NEWTON'S FIRST LAW

Newton's first law tells us that objects like to keep doing what they've been doing—whether moving or staying still. A skateboard won't move unless someone pushes it with their foot. But once the skateboard gets moving, it's hard to stop it.

Pushing something heavy, like a loaded shopping cart, takes effort. Once it's moving though, it doesn't take as much effort to keep moving it.

Objects like the cart or the skateboard have a fascinating force called **inertia**. Inertia happens when the object wants to keep doing what it's been doing whether moving or staying still.

When the Mystery Machine comes to a sudden stop, Scooby and the gang jerk forward for a moment. They keep moving even as the car stops. That's inertia at work!

### FACT

Inertia depends on the mass of the object. It takes more inertia to get Scooby rolling on a skateboard than his pint-size nephew, Scrappy-Doo!

## NEWTON'S SECOND LAW

As Scooby-Doo rides down a ramp on his skateboard, he keeps going faster and faster. In science-speak, he is accelerating. Acceleration is how fast something speeds up or slows down. The amount of speed depends on the force acting on the object and its mass.

To start going down the ramp, Scooby applies a force. He kicks off with his foot—er, paw. Newton discovered that the board's acceleration is equal to the force applied to it. In other words, the harder Scooby kicks, the faster he goes.

Scooby-Dooby Doo!

In another example, the harder you kick a ball, the farther it travels. But the heavier or bigger the ball is, the slower it will accelerate. Newton's second law shows us that the amount of force is mass **multiplied** by acceleration.

# NEWTON'S THIRD LAW

Have you ever tried bouncing a ball against the ground? If you push down hard, the ball bounces back up. The ground pushes the ball back into the air—an action and a reaction.

When you're swimming, you push the water back and the water pushes you forward. When you jump, you push down with your feet, and the ground pushes you upward.

These are examples of Newton's third law at work! This law shows us that forces come in pairs. When you push at something, it pushes back.

### FACT

When Shaggy skates down a ramp on his board, he has **momentum**. This is his mass in motion. The greater the mass, the more the momentum.

# Balloon Rocket Experiment

**WHAT YOU'LL NEED:**

scissors
straw
string
2 chairs
balloon
tape

**WHAT TO DO:**

1. Using the scissors, cut the straw into about 2-inch (5-centimeter) pieces.
2. Cut a length of string that is about 6 feet (1.8 meters) long.
3. Tie an end of the string to one of the chairs. Then slide one piece of straw onto the string.
4. Tie the other end of the string to the second chair.
5. Blow up the balloon. Pinch the end closed, but don't tie it.
6. Tape the side of the balloon to the straw. Make sure the pinched opening is at the back.
7. Pull the straw and balloon to one end of the string.
8. Release the balloon, and watch the rocket blast off!

## WHAT HAPPENED?

This experiment is a great way to see Newton's third law in action. The balloon releases air backward, which pushes the straw forward along the string. The action of letting the air out of the balloon created an equal and opposite reaction in the movement forward.

# CHAPTER 2
# Show of Force

What is force? Forces, like pushing or pulling, make things move. A force can stop something from moving too. We know that a skateboard that isn't moving needs a force to act on it.

The skateboarder pushes off the ground with a foot. This push is a force. This force makes the skateboard move.

But there are other forces that make sure the skateboard doesn't go flying off into space. If you threw a ball and there were no forces acting against its movement, the ball would keep going forever!

One force that slows the ball is gravity. Gravity is a force that pulls everything toward the center of Earth. Gravity keeps you from floating away.

# Egg Drop Experiment

## WHAT YOU'LL NEED:

bubble wrap

straws

cotton balls

cardboard box

tape

1–2 eggs

## WHAT TO DO:

1. Gather your materials: bubble wrap, straws, cotton balls, a cardboard box, and tape.
2. Use the materials listed above to build a protective structure for your egg. Get creative with your design!
3. Tape the structure securely to hold everything in place.
4. Once you're ready, drop the egg from up high, like from chair or stepladder. (Be sure to ask an adult for permission first.)
5. Check to see if the egg survived the fall. If it cracked, think about how you can improve your design—and then try again with a new egg.

Newton's three laws of motion are at work in this experiment. First, the egg is at rest until you drop it from a high place. The egg has inertia until it is dropped. As the egg falls, it accelerates toward the floor because gravity pulls it to the ground. The structure that you've built should protect it from the sudden stop.

One way to keep the egg safe is to slow down the drop. You could use air resistance to do this by making a parachute. You could also use soft materials to cushion the fall. This will absorb some of the force, keeping the egg from cracking.

Just like a science detective, keep thinking of other ways to make sure the egg doesn't break!

Another egg-cellent egg-speriment!

Another force is **friction**. Friction is a force that slows the movement of things when they rub against each other. Friction always acts in the opposite direction of movement.

When you walk, your feet rub against the ground, making friction. That friction prevents you from falling over.

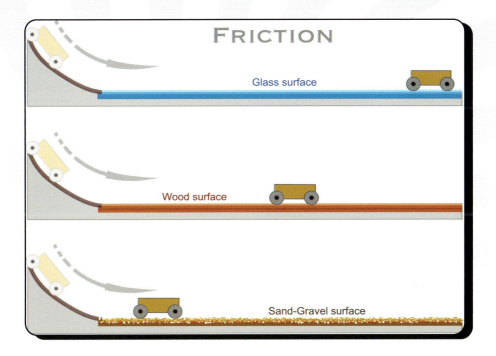

Friction slows a skateboard down as the wheels rub against the ground. Rough surfaces have more friction than smooth ones.

Pushing and pulling are also forces that make things move or stop moving. When someone pushes you on a swing, the force makes you fly high. When you're pulling a wagon full of Scooby Snacks, the pulling force makes the wagon move forward. When you push or pull an object, it pulls and pushes back with the same amount of force.

Which of Newton's laws talk about that?

**FACT**

**Lubricants** like oil can reduce the amount of friction. In a car engine, friction causes wear and tear. Lubricants help keep the engine going.

# CHAPTER 3
# Life in Motion

Forces and motion happen all the time in our daily lives. When we are walking, our feet push against the ground, which creates a force to move us forward. Gravity and friction keep us on the ground and prevent us from slipping.

Driving is a great example of forces and motion at work. By pushing the accelerator in a car, a driver creates a force that moves the car forward. Brakes slow the car down. Tires have **treads** that increase friction, so the car doesn't slip and slide.

Forces and motion are seen all the time in sports. A ballplayer hits a ball with a baseball bat. The harder they swing, the farther the ball goes. Gravity eventually brings the ball back to the ground. Friction on the ground slows the ball down until it comes to a complete stop.

At a construction site, forces and motion are always at work too. A crane lifting a heavy load high into the air uses force to overcome gravity. The greater the mass of the load, the greater the force needed to move it.

In each of these examples, a force is applied to the object that generates motion.

# CHAPTER 4
# Physics at Work

Riding a skateboard is a great example of the laws of physics at work. When the board is at rest, it has inertia. To overcome that, skateboarders learn how to make it move and keep balance. They also have to be aware of different surfaces that may trip them or winds that may blow them off.

When skateboarders push off, they accelerate. The harder they push off, the faster they go. The more mass they have, the more force is needed.

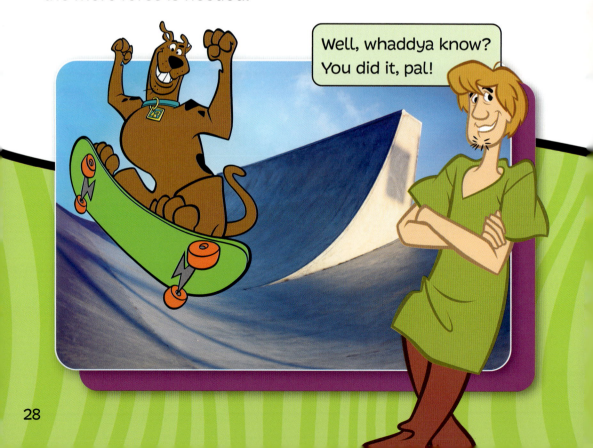

An expert skateboarder can push down on the board's tail, which launches them up into the air. When they land, they push down on the ground. The ground pushes back with an equal amount of force.

Can you see how Newton's three laws of motion have worked here? Can you think of other activities that show the laws of physics? Remember, gang, the mysteries of science are everywhere!

# GLOSSARY

**acceleration** (ak-sehl-uh-RAY-shun)—change in speed

**friction** (FRIK-shun)—the resistance of a surface to motion of an object moving over it

**gravity** (GRAV-uh-tee)—the force by which all objects in the universe are attracted to each other; Earth's gravity pulls objects toward the ground/its center

**inertia** (ih-NUR-shuh)—the way an object usually keeps doing what it's doing, either staying still or moving

**lubricant** (LOO-bri-kant)—any material such as oil, graphite, or grease that is used to coat closely fitting moving parts and thereby lower friction

**mass** (MAS)—the amount of matter in an object that gives it its weight

**momentum** (moh-MEN-tum)—the property of a moving object that determines how long it will take to stop, depending on its mass and speed

**multiply** (MUL-tuh-ply)—to increase the number, degree, or amount of

**tread** (TREHD)—the pattern of grooves on a tire or the depth of the grooves

# READ MORE

Colón, Erica L. *Awesome Physics Experiments for Kids: 40 Fun Science Projects & Why They Work!* New York: Callisto Kids, 2019.

Sohn, Emily. *A Crash Course in Forces and Motion with Max Axiom, Super Scientist.* North Mankato, MN: Capstone, 2019.

Turner, Myra Faye. *Discovering Forces and Motion in Max Axiom's Lab.* North Mankato, MN: Capstone, 2024.

# INTERNET SITES

*American Museum of Natural History: OLogy: Physics*
amnh.org/explore/ology/physics

*Ducksters: Physics for Kids*
ducksters.com/science/physics

*Kids Discover: Force and Motion*
online.kidsdiscover.com/unit/force-and-motion

# INDEX

acceleration  12

action, 9, 14, 17

force, 7, 9, 11, 12, 13, 18–19, 21–23, 24–27, 28–29

friction, 22–23, 24–25

gravity, 19, 24, 26–27

inertia, 11, 20, 28

mass, 9, 11, 12, 13, 15, 27, 28

momentum, 15, 30

motion, 5, 6–9, 15, 20, 22, 24–27, 29

Newton, Sir Isaac, 8

Newton's laws of motion, 9

physics, 5, 8, 28, 29

reaction, 9, 14, 17

resistance, 21

sports, 26

# ABOUT THE AUTHOR

Ailynn Collins has written many books for children, from stories about aliens and monsters, to books about science, space, and the future. These are her favorite subjects. She lives outside Seattle with her family and five dogs. When she's not writing, she enjoys participating in dog shows and dog sports.